Storm's Eye

Poems by
Judith Nicholls

Illustrated by Shirley Felts

Oxford University Press
Oxford New York Toronto

Other Oxford books by Judith Nicholls

Earthways Earthwise
Wish You Were Here?

Oxford University Press, Walton Street, Oxford OX2 6DP
Oxford New York Toronto
Delhi Bombay Calcutta Madras Karachi
Kuala Lumpur Singapore Hong Kong Tokyo
Nairobi Dar es Salaam Cape Town
Melbourne Auckland Madrid

and associated companies in
Berlin Ibadan

Oxford is a trade mark of Oxford University Press
Copyright © Judith Nicholls 1994
First published 1994
Illustrations © Shirley Felts 1994
ISBN 0 19 276127 7 (hardback)
ISBN 0 19 276138 2 (paperback)

All rights reserved. No part of this publication may be reproduced, stored in a retrieval system, or transmitted, in any form or by any means, without the prior permission in writing of Oxford University Press. Within the U.K., exceptions are allowed in respect of any fair dealing for the purpose of research or private study, or criticism or review, as permitted under the Copyright, Designs and Patents Act 1988, or in the case of reprographic reproduction in accordance with the terms of the licences issued by the Copyright Licensing Agency. Enquiries concerning reproduction outside those terms and in other countries should be sent to the Rights Department, Oxford University Press, at the address above.

A CIP catalogue record for this book is available from the British Library

Printed and bound in Great Britain by
Butler & Tanner Ltd, Frome and London

For John Foster,
with thanks.

Contents

Forest End
Since they left the house . . .

7	Forest End
8	Cockroach
8	Bluebottle
9	The Worm's Tale
10	Who am I?
11	Polar Cub
11	Kangaroo Haiku
12	Riddle
12	Monkey
13	Dragonbirth
14	Dragon Night
16	Dragon Days
17	Last Dragon
17	Tyrannosaurus Rex
18	Moth

Forty-one
Nobody knows just what goes on . . .

19	Forty-One
21	Mrs McQueen
22	Digger Daley
24	Moving In!

Beginnings
The three were a family . . .

27	Beginnings
28	A Lincolnshire Childhood
30	Mariage à la Mode
31	Transformations
32	Holly Berry
32	First Television
34	Science, 1953
36	Jerusalem
37	The Over-Reacher
38	Family Tree

Reaching Out
You're starting school . . .

39	New Beginnings . . .
40	Reading Time
41	What Andrew Did

42	What Can You Do With A Pencil?
43	Ars Mathematica
44	Giant Tale
46	Bell Boy
46	Bully
47	Grudges
48	He Loves Me, He Loves Me Not . . .
49	Miss Willis, PE
50	Personal

Before we are silenced . . .
Mummy, what was an elephant?

51	What Is One?
51	Firelight
52	Elegy
53	Future Past
53	Circus Elephant
54	Squirt!
55	Elephant
55	Bamboozled!
56	Wasp
58	What On Earth?
59	Stonehenge
61	Riddle
61	Slick Monster
62	Sealsong

Storm's Eye
The waiting waves still whisper . . .

63	Starfish
63	Goodwin Sands
64	SS Titanic
67	Eye of the storm
69	Cnut
72	La Baleine

Moving On
Dance to the song of the rains . . .

73	Train Ride
73	Puffing Billy
74	Haiku for Autumn
74	West Wind
75	Christmas Eve
75	Christmas Morning
76	Ballad of the Christchild
77	The Arrival of the Envelopes
79	The Coming of the Well
80	Shadows
80	Lotus

Forest End

Since they left the house . . .

Forest End

Since they left the house
the trees moved in;
the oak and ash made a home.
Where the chimney stood
is a jagged pine,
and the roof has almost gone.

Since they left the house
the birds moved in;
you can hear the thrush's song.
The house awakes
to the squawk of rooks,
and sleeps when the owl has flown.

Since they left the house
the winds moved in;
the windows wail and groan.
A few stairs creak
to a clouded sky,
then the house is left, alone.

Cockroach

Scuttle-bug,
shadow-foot,
bringer of night;
sky without stars,
obsidian-light;
shiny as coal,
new-mined and still bright;
smooth as new carbon,
dark and untyped.

Bluebottle

Who dips, dives,
swoops out of space,
a buzz in his wings
and sky on his face;
now caught in the light,
now gone without trace,
a sliver of glass,
never still in one place?

Who's elusive as pickpocket,
lord of the flies;
who moves like a rocket,
bound for the skies?
Who's catapult, aeroplane,
always full-throttle?
Sky-diver, Jumping Jack,
comet, *bluebottle*!

The Worm's Tale

'Women from St Teresa's Cheshire Home near Penzance, Cornwall, beat 34 other teams in the 10th annual worm charming championships yesterday at Blackawton, South Devon. Three of the night staff . . . managed to lure 72 worms from their 12 ft. square plot in the 15 minutes allowed. "The secret of our success was the worm song we sang constantly and the cold tea we poured on the ground," said Ms Allan, team captain . . .'
The Guardian, May 1993.

Dew sinks through the darkness,
dissolves like snow
into this private land of night.

I am no stranger to the gloom.
Here below
my pace is measured:
a gracious minuet
danced between roots of bindweed.
Here I could weave for ever
the dark fabric of my life;
here I could stay.

I have felt before
earth shake as thunder rolls,
the steady fall of rain on stone.
I have no fear.

And yet, today
I am aware of something
more insistent than a storm,
more haunting than a shower;
a watery almost-spell,
calling . . .

I turn,
lifted by music;
drawn, like Lazarus,
from the night.
Slowly I twist and rise
towards the day;
slowly I spiral out of darkness
into light.

Who am I?

I am the oldest of the bears
but I will never die!
I wander slowly, silently
beneath the midnight sky.

I am the largest of the bears;
I cannot sleep or fly,
and yet I rest above the clouds
and dance when the moon is high.

I am the farthest of the bears:
beyond the sun I lie!
I wander with a million stars . . .

I'm the Great Bear in the sky!

Polar Cub

This way, that way?
Step out,
little five-toe flat-foot,
squint-eye,
cave-dazed,
into the sun!

*Eyes left,
ears right,
nose to the wind!*

The coast is clear!
Run, roll, lollop;
winter's done!
Enjoy the pause;
make your mark
on this blank page –
the world is yours!

Kangaroo Haiku

Out of the forest,
on to the dry plain you spring,
light with grassy dreams.

Riddle

I am
pear-drop,
space-hopper,
rest-on-a-tail;
fast as a rocket,
and what's in my pocket
small as a snail?
I'm shorter than elephant,
taller than man;
I hop-step-and-jump
as no creature can.
My jacket is fur,
my pocket is too;
a joey hides there . . .
I am

      KANGAROO!

Monkey

I am
swing-on-a-tail,
up with the sun
fast as white lightning
slits skies at noon.
Now under palms,
now over fern;
dawn-creeper, branch-leaper,
dive, twist and turn.
Face-in-the-forest,
chasing the moon;
tree-lover, sky-brother,
dew-dancing one.

Dragonbirth

*In the midnight mists
of long ago
on a far-off mountainside
there stood
a wild oak wood . . .*

In the wild, wet wood
there grew an oak;
beneath the oak
there slept a cave
and in that cave
the mosses crept.
Beneath the moss
there lay a stone,
beneath the stone
there lay an egg,
and in that egg
there was a crack.
From that crack
there breathed a flame;
from that flame
there burst a fire,
and from that fire

dragon came.

Dragon Night

A dragon creeps
into my head
and wanders,
stealthy as a moon,
when day is left behind.
At dead of night,
as light as air,
as dark as lead
she sneaks,
in silence;
creeps into my head,
into my mind.

A dragon prowls
into my mind
and presses,
silent as a star,
into my dreams.
When day is left behind,
on padded feet
she treads through darkness,
pressing, pressing,
silently she presses
through the forests
of my mind.

A dragon roars
into the night,
hurls flames,
as fiery as a sun,
before my eyes, behind;
scours shadows into life
and thunders, panting
fire that sets alight

the forests of my dreams.
The dragon roars
into my night,
into my mind.

Dragon Days

*What did the dragon do all day
when he stepped out from the story-book?*

He chased a pretty princess
through a dark, dark wood;
he fought a gallant knight or two
to get a little food;
he ate a young girl's granny
just to show that he still could,
when he stepped out from the story-book.

*Oh, look! Put him back, back, back!
Put him in the story-book!*

*What did the dragon do all day
When he stepped out from the story-book?*

He scaled a castle wall
and lit a blacksmith's forge;
he strode around a mountain
and he leapt across a gorge,
then he found that he had landed
face to face with good St George,
when he stepped out from the story-book.

*Oh, look! Put him back, back, back!
Put him in the story-book!*

Last Dragon

By a dusk-damp cave
as the first snows fall
a dragon breathes;
the last of them all.

His eyes are dull,
his memories old;
his breath is pale,
his fire now cold.

The forest mice
who ran from his roar
now nest by his feet,
afraid no more.

He turns his face
to the winter moon;
his claws are furled,
his courage gone.

The first owl swoops
to the forest floor;
but the last of the dragons
is no more.

Tyrannosaurus Rex

So,
tyrannosaurus,
giant-jaw,
saw-teeth,
lash-o'-the-tail,
rip-o'-the-claw...

Who said *you* were king?

Moth

Fly-by-night,
moon-brusher,
searcher of light;
flibbertigibbet,
translunar kite.
Now a leaf,
now a message,
silent in flight:
wisp of torn paper
that drifts out of sight
then lifts in the wind
and is lost
to the night.

Forty-one

Nobody knows just what goes on . . .

Forty-One

The door is locked,
the curtains drawn;
the paint has peeled
from years of sun.
But there's no one dare
play 'knock and run'
or stand and stare
at forty-one!

For old Mr Dunn
of forty-one
is never seen
till the sun has gone.

There's no letter-box
at forty-one;
no postman knocks
for Mr Dunn.
There's nobody knows
just what goes on
in the silent rooms
of forty-one.

For old Mr Dunn
of forty-one
is never seen
till night has come.

'There's *nobody* there
at forty-one!'
some may declare;
but I know they're wrong.
For a grey cat prowls
across the lawn
and I've seen a light
where the curtain's torn;
and a shadow creeps
beneath the moon
when midnight strikes
at forty-one.

*For old Mr Dunn
of forty-one
steals out of his house
when midnight's come* . . .

Mrs McQueen

She keeps a pet peacock
to chase off black cats;
she walks under ladders,
steps on all cracks.

She opens her brolly
inside the front door;
she won't cross her fingers,
says it's a bore!

Her mirror is crazed
as an egg in a cup;
on her door hangs a horseshoe –
bottom-side up.

Her vases are filled
with sweet-smelling may
and six peacock feathers
stare from her bay.

She throws away wishbones,
won't have mistletoe;
buys lucky mince pies –
to feed her pet crow.

Born on a Friday,
one dark Hallowe'en;
she moved on St Swithin's
dressed all in green.

She's all right *so* far
from what I have seen –
but *I* would touch wood
if I lived at Thirteen!

Digger Daley

Digger Daley sleeps all night
but he's out at the stroke of eight.
'What I need is a great big hole:
a big square hole for a load of coal,
a hole for a pond and a hole for a fence,
a hole for a pole to keep in a foal,
and a hole for a post for the garden gate!'

Down on his knees
beneath the trees
he claws away at the earth;
a hand or a spade
and a new hole's made
as he digs for all he's worth.

Digger Daley digs all day
right to the stroke of eight.
'All I need is a small round hole:
a small round hole for an old lame mole,
a hole for a prop for a clothes-line pole,
a hole for a foal and a hole for a goal
and a hole for a post for the garden gate.'

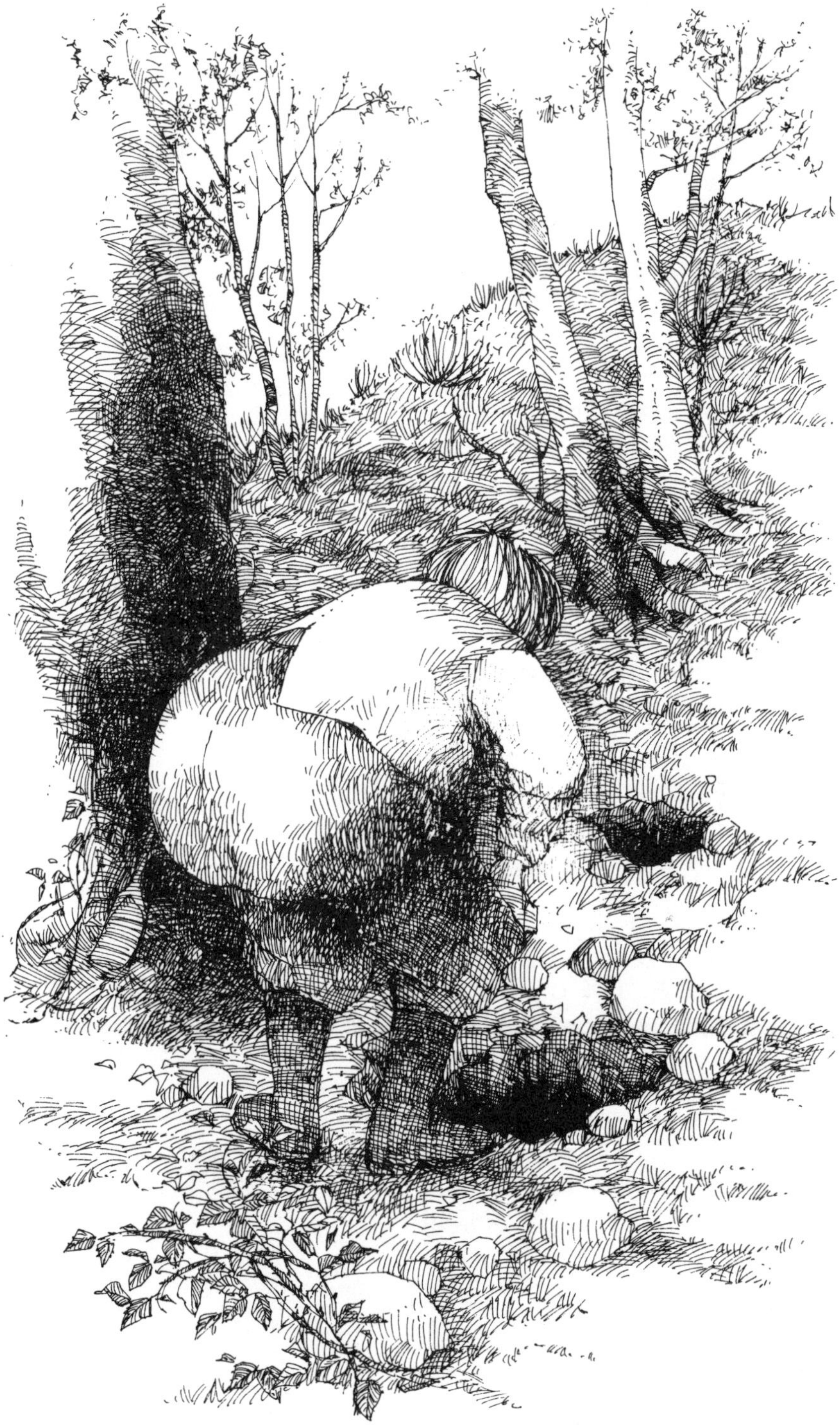

Moving In!

(For David Attenborough, in admiration!)

*The day that David moved next door
the neighbours stayed inside;
each one stared with baited breath,
as they flung the van doors wide . . .*

*But not a single table,
nor cupboard, chest, or drawers
no carpet, curtain, kettle, chair
was carried through those doors.*

First they let the ferret out,
then a sleepy sloth,
followed by a jackal–
intent on eating both!

Botfly, termite, aphid,
rush towards the house;
owl and fowl and ox and fox,
natterjack and mouse.

Cassowary, cockatiel,
partridge, pipit, quail
fill the air with squeak and squeal
to drown the peacock's wail.

'Now something's missing,' David mused.
'Have you seen my cat?'
Tiger growled and licked his lips –
from the neighbour's mat.

25

From an upstairs window
peer two old giraffes;
python slithers through the grass,
hyena bays and laughs.

On they rush towards the door:
puffin, prairie dog,
sewer-rat, mosquito, gnat,
orinoco hog . . .

David, deep in dust and dung
and skunks and trunks and feet,
sighed ecstatically and cried,
'I'm going to like this street!'

Beginnings

The three were a family . . .

Beginnings

In the beginning
was one.
Crouched in a cave
where bats first hung,
where webs were first woven,
dreams first spun,
crouched one,
alone.

And then one day
into the gloom
another came;
the fire was lit
the cave was warmed,
the howl of the wind
became a song
and two
were one.

Soon winter passed,
and into the sun
from the dark of the cave
one summer dawn
crept three:
the third was a child in arms,
the three were a family, new-born.

A Lincolnshire Childhood

She seldom left the house,
my grandmother.
Oh, she padded to the barn,
gave orders to my father,
worn from sawing musty logs –
and even bats lay low
above her thankless tongue,
rising in twilight musk.
Only her step was muffled
by slippers, sought each Christmas
worn inside and out.
Shoes stayed paper-stuffed,
reserved for funerals and the like,
no doubt.

Monday brought steaming sheets
and tempers, brandished dollylegs
and mangled bloomers,
chaste from copper tubs.
Twin lav, piled high
with last month's dusty *Mail*s,
was once more freshly-scrubbed,
though even Co-op bristles
never quite removed
the stench of chamber pots.

Linen sheets, now peasant white,
flounced boldly, barn to wall;
inside, zinc bath
half-full of pan-warmed water
circled child and man alike.
And half a lifetime on
they shiver,

wait in silent childhood dreams
the drama of her entrances.

('Dollylegs' can now be seen in folk museums: a kind of small wooden stool with four legs on the end of a long-handled stick. They were used to agitate the washing in the huge copper boiler.)

Mariage à la Mode

She made a good wife, my Aunt Sylvie.
With her curing hams and butter churn,
clocks glass-domed against a century's turn,
the waft of cooling milk or rising bread . . .
tight-lipped Victoria herself could earn
no better praise for thrift
or life well-led.

How would she see me now, piercing
with laser eye and sharper tongue
the wasted peelings, scribbled
'Try the freezer, dear, must go!' . . .
fast-forward entrances and partings,
whilst the weeds and ironing grow?

Lean, tight-bunned
with coil of grey which never fell
(*was* she once a girl, Aunt Sylvie?)
even at rest she firmly rocked
behind pursed lip and needle-click,
knitting thick socks with love
and pleasure – of a kind.

How would she see
the ready beans, pale chickens
plastic-clad and featherless;
tin-opener, out-of-season lettuces
and packets of square fish?

Tempus fugit
glints her grey-faced clock.
Unseen, she fills the gloom
and watches, silenced,
by the Hogarth prints.

Transformations

'Well, well, we've grown!'
My uncle,
stubble-chinned,
nails blackened by
a lifetime in the fields
of furrowed Lincolnshire.
Hair roughly stacked
on wind-pocked face;
few words, though
'How you've grown!'
served well enough to raise
a childish moan.

Some ten years on,
the stubble thinned,
knuckles deeper-ploughed
with black on brown.
Words, much the same;
stoop, lower; face,
furrowed. And ten years on
at least I have the grace
on hearing how I've grown
to hold my tongue
and still the childish moan.

Another dozen years;
my uncle, teeth and stubble gone,
lies pale behind his boyish fears.
No words, no nod;
the old man dreams alone
knowing now, perhaps,
his growing's done.
And I, with children of my own,
now turn to them and smile
to hear again their echoes
of my childish song.

Holly Berry

My holly-berry lay
as red as the sun
that shines in a summer sea;
I sowed my berry
when I was young
to make me a holly tree.

My holly-berry grew
to a holly bush
just half as tall as me:
my days were long,
there was no rush
to see my holly tree.

Now I am old
and years have gone
since it first stood over me;
but my holly grows on,
still straight, still strong,
a shining holly tree.

First Television

It was 1953.
My dad had won the pools:
some pounds and shillings spare!
He'd buy our first TV.

*Coronation coming up,
chance of a lifetime!*
he cried excitedly.
I never thought we'd see!

And he,
abandoning his much-loved wireless,
settled down to dream in black and white
of London pomp.

On Coronation Day
I did begin to watch,
to please my dad . . .

But back in school,
to celebrate, they'd handed out
free tickets for the fair.
It wasn't long before
I grew impatient,
tired of moving images,
seen from a lolling chair.
And drawn instead by dodgems,
ghost trains, candy floss,
I walked out on those early pictures
snatched from air.

Science, 1953

It was called Domestic Science then.
Formica no more heard of than moon travel,
Beatles, tights or Home Econ.,
each wooden table must be scrubbed
(scrubbed hard and long)
after each shapeless pasty,
limp cucumber sandwich,
had earned its sad D+
from school, and later home.
To me they tasted fine.

Miss explained that only *tops*
of frying pans required a shine,
as blackened bottoms drew more heat.
Highly scientific, so we thought,
but not my mother.
Slapdash and dirty, she's a fool,
my mother muttered, crossly
brandishing wire wool.

She was not noted for her scientific flair;
I less still for my domestic skill.
Yet three domesticated decades on
I live with blackened proof
that science won.

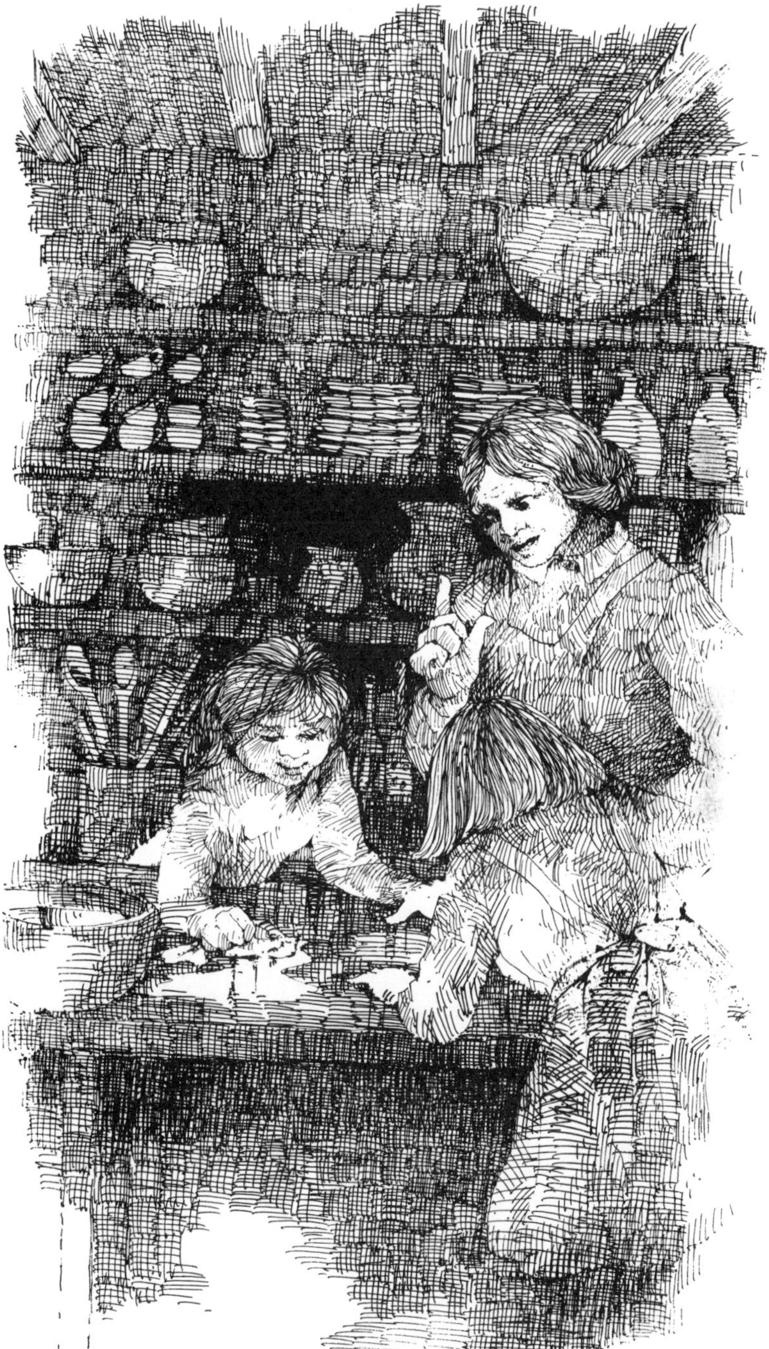

Jerusalem

'You love this boy?'
My stern headmaster spoke.
'I – like him, sir. A lot.'
A late October heat
rose from the polished oak,
invaded feet and breast,
pressed hard against my tie.
Nearby a first-year singing class,
my green-clad images, strain,
summon again a green and pleasant past
from England's clouded hills,
promise in vain
Jerusalem.

Eyes fall,
bury a summer's dream
beneath the green-gold tie
and buttoned gabardine.
Satchel, weathered
through a seven-year quest,
hides in sham decency
an unquiet world of books:
of Cleopatra's lust,
Othello's green-eyed monster,
anguished Tess.

'You– "like" him.'
His silence chills,
and yet his eyes
belie the stillness of his face.
He understood, perhaps,
we meddled in a dangerous world;
he ruled an age of prefects, ties and caps
yet passion lurked beneath the green and gold.

The Over-Reacher

You can do anything, my father said;
A challenge to my childish pride, no threat.
His words will blindly dog me till I'm dead.

For forty years enmeshed within my head
I carried this and cast out far my net.
You can do anything, my father said.

Searching, unsatisfied by daily bread
I sweated on, unwilling to forget;
His words will blindly dog me till I'm dead.

My body gave a caveat: just tread
With caution, you can't walk on water yet.
You can do anything, my father said.

Becalmed in doldrum age, no longer fed
With pestering pride he rests; for me the debt.
His words will blindly dog me till I'm dead.

How many years I wished those words unsaid;
Too late to change, may flesh still live to fret.
You can do anything, my father said;
His words will blindly dog me till I'm dead.

Family Tree

I am
the family tree.
Before time barely had begun
I rooted,
splintering frozen stone.

I am
the family tree.
Through fire and ice I've crept and crawled,
roots stretching wider,
branches tall.

I am
the family tree.
Those roots, now laced in ancient moss,
still feed young branches
grasping into space.

I am their base;
I am your base.

Reaching Out

You're starting school . . .

New Beginnings . . .

You're starting school! my mother said.
You'll read and write and sew . . .
But I can read at home, I cried.

Big girls all go!

You'll love the boys and girls, she said,
and all those games they play . . .
But I could stay and play at home!

Big girls don't stay!

I stood and stared through wooden gates
and watched her wave good-bye,
till sudden mist hid her from view . . .

Big girls don't cry!

Reading Time

*Please, Mrs Harris,
there's a bat
on the mat . . .*

Well read, Sue,
but right just now
I'm listening to . . .

*No, Mrs Harris,
I mean
there IS a bat
on the mat!*

Oh, a bat and *ball*!
Thank you, Sue,
just pick it up
and pop it in the hall
for PE time, can you?

*NO, Mrs Harris,
I mean a BAT,
just like I said.*

I think it might be dead.

*Shall I bring it here,
or will you come and . . .*

*OH, Mrs Harris, LOOK!
It ISN'T dead.
Can you see its furry head?
I think it's waking up!*

Mrs Harris . . . ?

What Andrew Did

You have twenty minutes to finish,
Miss Smith announced at 2.00.
I'd finished already and had a book
but I settled to watch Andrew . . .

Out of his seat and chatting
by 2.01 with Tim;
fiddling with a clay model
that wasn't made by him.
Conversation's louder
and time is pushing on;
2.08 when he sits down
to fiddle with his pen.
Is it work? Suspense is high . . .
but no, some rubbing out
and then a quiet sing with Tim
who's now doing walkabout.
2.16. A sentence done?
Ah, no, he's tying his lace;
now staring, gaping, fiddling
with Blu-Tack on his face.
2.18, scrapes back his chair
and writes on Gary's back;
laughs with Tim, kicks Philip's shin
then pelts him with Blu-Tack . . .

2.20, children, time is up!
First, Andrew, stand up please!
Stand up, speak up; let's all hear
YOUR lengthy masterpiece!

What Can You Do With A Pencil?

(For an unknown boy in Winchester!)

You can sharpen it
or break the point,
trap it in the door;
fasten it behind your ear
or *tap* it on the floor;
use it as a walking stick
(if you're very small),
dig a hole to plant a seed,
tap it on a wall;
use it as a handy splint
for rabbits' broken legs;
stir your coffee,
stir your tea,
stir up all the dregs!
Drop it from a table top,
pop it in a case;
use it as a lollystick,
send it up in space!
Two will give you chopsticks,
one could pick a lock;
bore a hole and thread one
to darn a hole-y sock . . .

These are just a few ideas,
there must be *hundreds* more . . .
but meantime, trap it, snap it, flap it,

TAP IT ON THE FLOOR!

Ars Mathematica

        Any
      triangle
with two equal angles
of however many degrees you please
will be known by the grand name of isosceles.

Parallelogram
not a problem
a rectangular
dipsomaniacal
quadrilateral.
Right angles?
Not necessary.
Systematical!
So ecstatical
problematical
box that I am,
Parallelogram!

        A
   square
is four-sided
completely right-angled
nothing new-fangled
or rare in a
square

A trapezium
Here is an easy one
two sides are parallel
this you can follow well
two more can be symmetrical
result can even be poetical!

Next
the hexagon
Here's a pesky one
six axes of symmetry
so handy in geometry
tessellates simply
polygon for
six

You have certainly seen a rectangle
if you've ever been in a quadrangle
four sides and equal sides opposite
four right angles, not my favourite

Giant Tale

He was . . .

As tall as a redwood,
wide as a willow;
his snore was the thunder,
a mountain his pillow.

Each step brought an earthquake,
each breath blew a gale;
one laugh moved an ocean,
each tear filled a pail.

His chin was Australia,
his elbow Bengal;
his nose was Mount Everest,
each tooth was a wall.

His mouth was a crater,
with snakes for a tongue;
his eyes were the size
of the earth and the sun.

One toe was as heavy
as Venus and Mars;
his forehead was Saturn,
his hair all the stars . . .

. . . *all the STARS?*
You're pulling my leg!

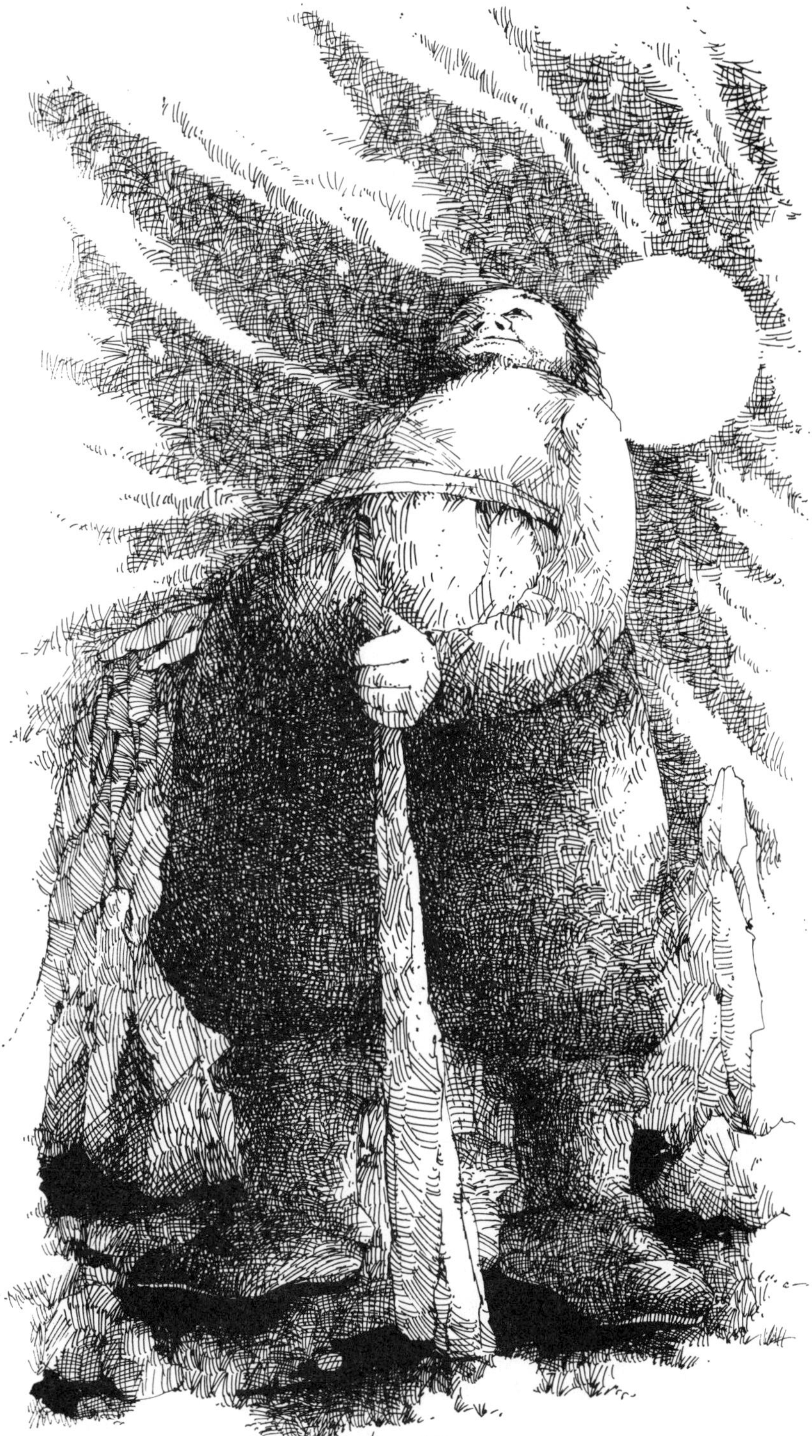

Bell Boy

Sir has got no favourites,
the long, the short or tall;
by three on Friday afternoon . . .
he loves us all!

Sir won't pick on anyone,
the ninny or the swat;
come the bell at three o'clock . . .
he loves the lot!

Sir is always super-fair
in any row or brawl,
but when the break-bell calls us out
he loves us best of all!

Sir's never mean to anyone,
you'll never hear a snub;
but hear the bell at twelve o'clock
and sir's off to the pub!

They say that sir can't care for us
or get much satisfaction . . .
but I know sir now pretty well,
and when he hears that hometime bell
he loves us to distraction!

Bully

Kevin Nuttall's a dreamer
and Gary Flynn's a fool;
Charlie Watt's the biggest swat
that ever walked the school.
Put Timmy Fitch on a football pitch
if you want to see him move,
but keep away from Jonathan Grey
                  – he's the Guv.

Sally Dee's ginger and freckled
and always good for laughs;
Andy can tell a good story
and Clare's Professor of Maths.
Marty Stubbs can outstare any teacher –
he's Mary Bollom's love.
But Jonathan Grey always gets his way
				– he's the Guv.

Mike Walder and Annie Bradford
can outrun anyone;
Chris Potts blows the fattest bubbles
on second-hand bits of gum.
Vicki is tough, with fist enough
to scare the roughest thug,
but Jonathan Grey they all obey
				– he's the Guv.

Grudges

It isn't fair . . .
that I must be in bed
for hours before,
that I get all the blame
and never her,
that she's allowed to choose
what she will wear,
it isn't fair!

It isn't right . . .
that she's allowed out
late at night,
that she can choose
when to switch off her light,
that I'm the one told off
whenever there's a fight,
it isn't right!

47

It makes me mad . . .
that they think she's so good
and I'm so bad,
that she gets extra cash
for helping Dad,
that her old coats are all
I've ever had,
it makes me mad!

*(I know I'm nine
and she is seventeen;
that's no excuse at all
for them to be so MEAN!)*

He Loves Me, He Loves Me Not . . .

(Sing to the tune of 'Bobby Shaftoe')

Peter Packer, he loves Dee,
but she chases Johnny Lea,
Johnny says that he loves me,
Poor old Peter Packer!

Peter Packer's not too clever,
Dee says she will love him never,
he says he'll love Dee for ever,
Potty Peter Packer!

Johnny Lea is chasing Dee now,
Dee has gone off Johnny Lea now,
Peter Packer's after me now,
Perfect Peter Packer!

Miss Willis, PE

With shorts in modest pleats,
well-pressed,
white shirt well-buttoned
(over aertex vest),
Miss Willis ruled the field.
Her hair, which longer
might have swung too wild,
lies cropped in regimented waves,
disorder unrevealed.

From light and even tan
(Miss Willis was not noted
for excess)
she summons us to heel;
in gym, on hockey field,
stares disbelieving
at our feckless limbs.
Refuses notes (well-forged)
for missing games or shower,
propels us with no mercy
to the high jump
or the double bar.

She fell
(if such was possible)
for some wee Scot,
a German teacher
half her size;
opted for teamwork (licensed)
and the marriage stakes –
her biggest hurdle
in our eyes.

Personal

Middle-aged male,
slightly balding,
one eye lost in battle
years ago, but copes.
Friendly nature,
uncomplaining.
Lives simply,
inexpensive tastes,
no ties.
Seeks good home, friendship,
view to permanent relationship.

Contact: Ed. Bear, Box 100.

Before we are silenced . . .

Mummy, what was an elephant?

What Is One?

One is the sun,
a rhino's horn;
a drop of dew,
a lizard's tongue.

One is the world,
a lonely whale;
an elephant's trunk,
a monkey's tail.

One is an acorn,
one is a moon;
one is a forest,
felled too soon.

Firelight

Last night
as flames curled round my coal
I thought I saw
a million years ago
a forest fall.

Elegy

'Mummy, what was an elephant?'

Each ear was tuned to the forest,
each trunk uncurled to the sun;
each forehead domed against a sky
unchanged since time began.

Each head was raised in greeting
as they swayed from each new dawn,
and the timeless paths of the forest
echoed with trumpet-song.

Now the skies are dark,
the paths have gone;
what once was a forest
has turned to stone.
Now only vultures
shadow the sky
and the queens of the forest
are left, to die.

Before we are silenced,
hear our song;
before we are silenced,
hear our cry.

Future Past

Lord of Africa,
swaying giant of the plains;
tree-mover,
sand-tosser,
diviner of water
from the dry river bed:
where are you now?

Where is the song on ivory keys
that echoed through the dusk?
The song's cut away
for a handful of beads
which once were a living tusk.
Now only baubles
glint in the sun,
for the forest lord fell
to the sound of a gun.

Circus Elephant

Today, I dance,
I tiptoe, sway,
with sawdust at my knees;
yesterday, lifetimes away,
I lumbered through the trees.

Squirt!

*What can an elephant
do with a trunk
when the sun is blazing hot?*

He can
take it for a walk
to the waterhole,
suck a little water up
to make him cool –
then squirt all over his back,
THAT'S WHAT!

When the sun is blazing hot?

OH YES,
he can squirt all over his back!

WHY NOT?

Elephant

Ocean of dry land,
sand-sprayed,
heaving spring-tide
lifted by the moon;
unhurried season's turn.

No tusk-etched image,
stumbled on at dawn
deep in some icy cave,
could show our children's children,
help them know
that great, slow, swaying
of a timeless past
before the guns were born.

Bamboozled!

A polar bear just loves an icy landscape,
The eagle likes a mountain with a view;
A whale demands an oceanful of water...
All *I* want is a thicket of BAMBOO!

The magpie gathers sticks and straw for nesting,
For a woodlouse some rotting bark will do;
The rabbit digs her home beneath the forest...
For *mine* I just need old stalks of BAMBOO!

Some tasty mouse is buzzard's choice for dinner,
A field of grass is what a cow will chew;
Koalas can't resist their eucalyptus...
All *I* need is a bunch of ripe BAMBOO!

Please!

Wasp

'They'll have to go!'
the neighbours said.
'They fly, they multiply,
they're into kitchens,
apples, pears, and blackberries . . .
my sister even found one in her bed!
If they stay now,
you've got them for the summer –
and a million more!
They'll have to go,' they said.

But killing's *wrong*!
still echoed through my head.
Live and let live.
What does it matter
if they share our eaves?
There's space for them to wander
as they please –
and plenty left for us.
But no; still they said,
'They'll have to go!'

'You have to kill at dusk,' they said.
'They work till light has gone.
You'll see them back and forth –
and then again at dawn.
But not at night.
You'll be all right,' they said.
'At dusk they all return,
you'll get them then.'

So as light faded,
out came helmet, boots and gloves,
scarf, long jacket, mask. And spray.

Ladder to the wall, planks
to span the small outbuilding roof
that leads right to the hole.
And all the time they flew,
not wasting any minute of their day.
Effortlessly, unarmed (almost),
they worked on through the dusk.

And then
we killed them.
Standing down below
I waited for resistance,
at least some sort of show –
defiance, anger, even panic,
I don't know.
I wanted them, somehow,
to let our neighbours know
that they weren't beaten yet;
to rise again, like dandelions
plucked from neat gardens,
only to carpet countless fields
in bursting May.
But there was nothing.
Darkness fell,
the planks were put away
and anxiously we listened.
From the still night air
came only
silence.

I thought of them again next day,
as I sat dreaming in the sun
and watched, with half-closed eyes,
small spiders spinning through my lawn.
Where had they fallen?

How many *might* have been?
And then I was aware
of some small sound.
Familiar, coming near.
Small draught above my ear;
slight brushing of the hair . . .
Then suddenly,
alighting boldly on my chair,
I saw him,

here!

What On Earth?

What on earth are we doing?
Once wood-pigeons flew,
and young badgers tunnelled
where oak and ash grew . . .

Now the forest's a runway,
and all that flies through
is a whining grey plane
where the pigeons once flew.

Where on earth are we going?
At the end of the lane
once blackberries hung
in soft autumn rain . . .

Now the lane is a car park,
and never again
will fruit fill our baskets
down in the lane.

Why on earth are we crying?
Once morning dew shone
on hawthorn and primrose,
caught in the sun . . .

Now the forest is carpeted
only with stone.
No primrose, no hawthorn;
the forest has gone.

Stonehenge

What would THEY think of it now . . .?

I wanted to walk to it, turf-ambling over miles of ageless
    green
to the sudden shock of silent discovery–
the achievement of real men in the face of real gods.
But no, I must drive my car purposefully
across the wreckage of modern technology:
of course we aren't allowed to discover it –
let us shield men from the shock of receiving any real impact.
Follow the signs along a sense-insulated under-passage,
don't forget to pay your twenty pence at the ticket office.
Ars longa, vita brevis . . .

What would THEY think of it now –
they, who laboured sun upon sun
to the glory of unknown gods –
that we pay twenty pence to ogle
in plastic picnic-beakered daylight
under the burr of hostile helicopters?

I should have come at dusk, or dawn.
But of course that can't be done;
not even twenty pence will raise the iron-fast gate
that might lead through to real experience.
Take your twenty pence worth of cheap sensation between
    9 and 5
glimpses of eternity first on the left and don't leave litter.

When THEY built it, there were no motorways
to dwarf it from infinity.
No hygienic kiosks with cellophaned sandwiches
and orange-coloured mush in tidy paper cups.
Only stars and gods.
Now we are afraid to live too close to the gods.
But this is supposed to be the age of Aquarius . . .?
Maybe our children . . .?

I would like to say a prayer at the altar of these ancient gods
that our children at least might live nearer the elements . . .
But the helicopter roars above, lorries
close in all around and a school party
with clicking cameras swarms between.
I turn away, commit the prayer
to the last solitude,
to the whispering air
and an unknown god.

Riddle

For want of a word
the thought was lost;
for want of a thought
the tree was lost;
for want of a tree
the forest was lost;
for want of the forest
a land was lost;
for want of a land
the people were lost;
and all for the want
of one small word . . .
                why?

Slick Monster

Velvet black wave
gently laps the shore;
small white seagull
flies no more.

Shiny black monster
slowly creeps to land;
small pink crab
buried in the sand.

Sealsong

Around me, seas
stretch endlessly;
above me, sky.
A space to breathe,
a place to swim;
to pace the days
by moon or sun.
A place that time
had kept from man;

no place to die.

Storm's Eye

The waiting waves still whisper . . .

Starfish

Went star-fishing last night.
Dipped my net in the inky lake
to catch a star for my collection.
All I did was splintered the moon.

Goodwin Sands

I have seen the pale gulls circle
against a restless sky;
I have heard the dark winds crying
as dusk-drawn clouds wheel by.

But the waiting waves still whisper
of shadowy ocean lands,
of twisting tides and of secrets
that lie beneath the Sands.

I have seen the wild weeds' tangle
and smelt the salted squall;
I have seen the moon rise from the seas,
and felt the long night's fall.

But whose are the voices that echo
from the shifting ocean lands,
that tell of secrets buried
beneath the drifting Sands?

For many sail the Goodwins
and some return to shore;
but others ride in the falling tide
and those are seen no more.

And voices rise from the waters
beneath a restless sky:
in the dying light of coming night
the long-lost sailors sigh;
from the watery lands of Goodwin Sands
I hear the sailors cry.

SS Titanic

15 April 1912

First was the silence. Not below,
where silver forks and laughter
chink in each saloon;
where layered decks of dance and song
echo through perfumed corridors,
all set to last till dawn.
Nor several tiers down
in simpler quarters.
There, for the first time ocean-borne,
emigrants still chatter,
more subdued in tone;
entrust to some far-off new world
their dreams
and all they own.

But high above the deck
is peace.
The wind is slight,
though air has chilled surprisingly:
little swell,
no waves to speak of,
movement smooth, unhampered.
The theatre set.
Viewed from the gods her course is clear,
pulled, as if by chains, on steady track
towards her destination.
Behind, the wake spreads endlessly,
stretches wide then slowly fades
into the night.

Only a faint jarring interrupts
that almost total silence of the sea,
barely noticed by the revellers.
There is no panic.
A brief encounter with an icy shelf
means nothing to a ship that is
unsinkable. . .

Later, she begins to list;
the rest is known.
Emigrants from flooded cabins
claw through dark companionways,
held back to save the rich;
lifeboats lowered quarter-full;
the shameless fights for precedence.

And for the rest,
gathering in disbelief on darkened decks,
the wait.
One weeps,

one lights a cigarette,
one goes below, changes to evening dress
to meet his fate.
On sloping decks the band play on –
Hold me up in high waters
their almost final line.

At last, she rises almost vertical –
a lifelong memory
for those who lived to tell the tale –
then slides, nose-first
towards her brave new world
encompassed only by
the lasting silence of the sea,
the silence of the sky.

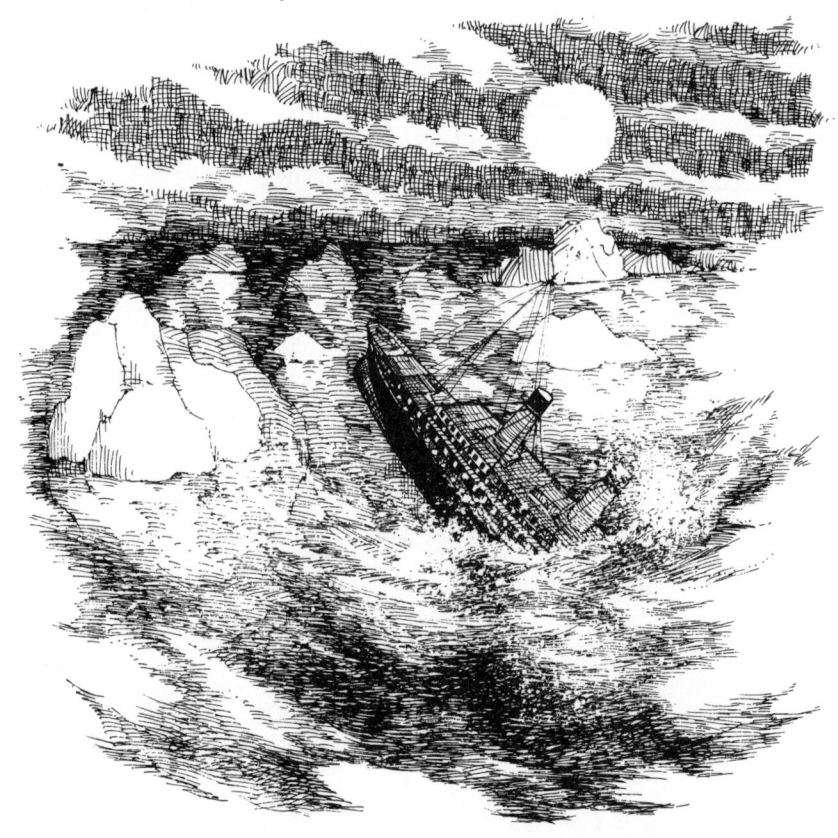

Eye of the storm

The great sea painter J.M.W. Turner once had himself lashed to a ship's mast in order to experience a storm at sea.

Spray lifts and hovers,
soon whisked white
from darkening seas.
Sails strain before the mast;
with each new gust
taut riggings groan.
Wind rises still,
prises eyelids open,
claws at cheeks and nostrils
sharp with salt.

Vertical is lost;
she rolls and pitches,
pitches, rolls.
And mast and man lurch on
as one, through sea and air;
through gloom then glare,
they twist into the staring eye
of Turner's first sea-storm.

Sky breaks all round;
green light dissolves grey noon,
day becomes night.
The weight of waters,
lava-angry,
churns beneath, around.
The seagulls' cry is lost
as ocean rises up to meet the sky.

Waves curve
and swell, mast-high,
to spinning walls

of foam and cloud and ocean.
Keel swerves and lifts,
dragged to the peak
then spewed down concave cliff
to beckoning trough beneath,
skewed in the undertow.

Gunwales dip to starboard,
mast falls, a hinging lid
to close the gaping sea below.
But no, she rises;
counter-balanced,
lists to port,
is tossed head-on,
the sport of some sea-god,
towards another wave
above the surging foam.

....

And he,
transfixed with fear and cold,
still stares.
Through artist's eye, salt-stung,
he fixes in his head
the green eye of the storm;
and even as his life is hurled
to places out of time,
where earth and sea and sky are one,
holds still the moving image in his soul;
later, recreates it whole
and pours it on to canvas
for the world.

Cnut

Great king,
just ruler of our forests,
wise ruler of our plains;
ruler of the wild winds
that safely blew our conquering sails;
ruler of cloud and sun,
ruler of the loud waters of the ocean,
of the quiet rivers,
of the sand;
there is no wolf or worm
no speck of dust,
no stone unturned
would not bow down
before your wise command.
The very storm, oh king,
for you would halt its icy breath;
the seas would leave the land!

These are foolish words
he gently sighed;
for I am just a man . . .

But still they fawned
and bowed and lied
and kissed obsequiously
his kingly hand:
The winds would halt,
the moon would fade,
and the forests leave our land;
the very tides would turn away
at our lord's first command!

Enough, I pray
of careless words!

I beg you, say no more!
Just carry my throne
to the salt-sea's edge
where the ocean meets the shore.

They carried his throne
to the salt-sea's edge
and they carried him on his throne;
and there, where the tide had almost ebbed
and the sand was damp and firm,
there, foolishly they waited
till the tide began to turn.

Let us lift you back,
oh wisest king;
back to the drier sand!
There is no need,
the king replied,
if I may just command!

The water rose
to toes, to heels;
they stood in disarray.
They stared, they whispered urgently
and wished the waves away.

The king was calm;
he raised his arm
and spoke out to the sea:
Go back, grey ocean;
back, slow tide!
And the water reached his knee.

Oh, just and wise,
the tide is strong;
we fear that you will drown!

And they made to lift him from the seas,
but he ordered,
Put me down!

They shivered, fearful;
he sat firm
and boldly raised his hand:
*Go back, grey ocean,
back, I say;
pray turn your tide
the other way!
I order, I COMMAND!*

The water gushed about his waist
and still the courtiers stood.
In tears they begged:
Let us take you back,
oh just king, wise and good!

He turned at last
as water lapped
and swirled towards his head;
*Now you may move me from the sea
to safe dry land,* he said.
*You may take me back
before we drown;
for now you understand
there is but One
can move the tides,
across the waiting sand.*

*There is but One
can move the tide
or still the storm-tossed wood.
Know only that I am your king –*

but I am not your God.

La Baleine

J'suis toujours danseuse
sur les vagues de la mer;
je saute au ciel,
j'suis pas de la terre!
Je vole, nuage au ciel . . .
puis je tombe,
pierre grise et lourde,
vers les sables profonds.

Whale

(rough translation)

I'm the eternal dancer
on the waves of the sea;
I leap to the sun,
I'm not of the earth!
I fly, a cloud in the sky . . .
then I fall,
a heavy grey stone,
towards the deep sands.

Moving On

Dance to the song of the rains . . .

Train Ride

Steam train
slides over tracks
through silent countryside;
a dark snake stalking through tall grass,
hissing.

Puffing Billy

Puffing Billy, built in 1813, is probably the world's oldest locomotive. It is now on permanent exhibition at the London Science Museum.

Sometime-dinosaur,
rattling hulk of bones
that lumbered once
through English green,
spelt death to ancient ways
in smoke-black breath.

Now anchored
on a one-way track to nowhere,
Penny Black of steam;
collected, shown
for all to gawp and say:
*He had his day,
those early engine-makers
knew their stuff.*

Now silenced, still
his last breath gone:
Tyrannosaurus Bill
run out of puff.

Haiku for Autumn

Hedgerows fired with beech,
lawn smouldering with apples;
golden October!

Silence pungent as
oranges, darkened summits
humped with wind-bared rock.

Rush of water over stone
and not-quite-silences
of wind through trees.

West Wind

roused us last night
with his roistering clatter,
rudely bursting through
latched windows
locked doors
without so much as a
'May I come in?'
or ring of the midnight bell

lifts curtains
rushes impatient
under doors,
swirls down chimneys
like some drunken
blustery Santa
lost in time.

Christmas Eve

Bedtime.
Curtains drawn now,
parents yawn. Children try
to still their racing thoughts, but sleep
has gone.

Christmas Morning

Open the stocking,
what's in there?
Five hazelnuts, an apple,
a tangerine, a pear.

Untie the ribbons,
what do you spy?
A pencil and a hanky,
a freshly-baked mince pie.

Take off the wrappings,
what can it be?
A clockwork car, a storybook,
a game of chess for me.

Look by the fireside,
what is that?
A box of paints, a jigsaw,
a red wool stripy hat.

Peep through the curtains,
who goes there?
Mary and her Baby,
and the Christmas star.

Ballad of the Christchild

What are you dreaming,
Oh tell me, fair Christchild,
As soft in your straw bed
You sleepily lie?

Is it of Mary,
The mother who watches?
Of shepherds who seek you
This first Christmas day?

Is it of wise men
Who travel from east lands,
Bringing their rich gifts
Of gold and of myrrh?

Or is it of Herod
Who seeks to destroy you
And yet has not followed
Your own single star?

Perhaps it's of palm trees
Which wave high before you,
Scatter the floor as you
Walk through the street?

The calls of 'Hosanna!'
Of men kneeling for you?
Is it for this, Child,
You stir in your sleep?

*What are you dreaming,
Oh tell me, fair Christchild,
Wreathed in the darkness
By warm oxen breath?*

*Sleep now, fair Christchild,
Rest in your stable;
Out of the darkness
Will come peace on earth.*

The Arrival of the Envelopes

Each Christmas they arrive,
drop guilt through my letter-box
like uninvited guests:
a festive season's tax
against excess.

Later, coffee-stained
among the shopping lists
they steal into my mind:
what price a baby,
out of sight
in some forgotten land . . .
or Christmas tree, a turkey, wine?
Uneasily I waver,
choices intertwined.

Next day I gather
in a rush of shame
worn shirts and unworn shoes
for Christmas sales;
cook leftovers,
walk into town.
Though skies are grey
I don't complain;
patiently, for once,
peg blankets out to dry,
remembering some child
with no wrap to his name
who waits, more patiently than I
beneath a different sky
for rain.

Each Christmas,
bellies overfed again
we reach, shame-faced
for cheque or purse.
Each Christmas we recall
with just a twinge of pain,
a child who lies,
belly distended,
with no crust to his name;
who starves,
who dies.

The Coming of the Well

Our fields have gone,
the days burn on;

Cry for the sigh of the rains!

The days burn on;
beneath that sun

Long for the lash of rain!

Beneath the sun
with swollen tongue

Beg for the roar of the rain!

With swollen tongue,
though no words come

Pray for the whisper of rains!

Though no words come
and days burn on,
beneath our land,
still crazed by sun,

Hear the song of the rains!

*Though no rains come
and days burn on,
beneath our land
we hear that song;*

*Hear the song of the rains.
Dance to the song of the rains!*

Shadows

Stand with your back
to the shining sun;
watch your shadow
dance and run.

Stand and face
the shining sun;
look ahead–
your shadow's gone!

Lotus

Though each of my roots
in darkness was born
yet will I reach for the light,
yet will I rise to the sun.